INSIDE CRIME

INS

FORENSICS

Colin Hynson

W

FRANKLIN WATTS

LONDON • SYDNEY

First published in 2010 by
Franklin Watts
338 Euston Road
London NW1 3BH

Franklin Watts Australia
Level 17/207 Kent Street
Sydney NSW 2000

Series editor: Jeremy Smith
Editors: Sarah Ridley and Julia Bird
Design: sprout.uk.com
Artworks: sprout.uk.com
Picture researcher: Diana Morris

A CIP catalogue record for this book is available
from the British Library.

ISBN 978 0 7496 9584 2

Dewey classification: 363.2'5

Printed in China

Franklin Watts is a division of Hachette Children's
Books, an Hachette UK company.
www.hachette.co.uk

CONTENTS

INSIDE PICTURE

Forensic scientists perform a vital role in the fight against crime. They use their scientific knowledge and expertise to investigate crimes by looking at evidence at crime scenes and taking evidence back for further work in the laboratory. Forensic evidence is often used in criminal trials and can help prove someone's guilt – or their innocence.

At the scene of a crime

For forensic scientists it is very important that the scene of a crime is 'secured' as soon as possible. This means that the crime scene is quickly closed off to everybody except those who are authorised to enter. Forensic scientists record everything at the scene that may be relevant to the crime. This might involve taking measurements, writing down notes, taking photographs or selecting evidence to take back to the laboratory.

ON TARGET

In Britain the police force uses a government-owned business called the Forensic Science Service (FSS) to provide their forensic services. The FSS employs 1,300 people. They attend over 1,500 crime scenes and work on 120,000 criminal cases every single year. They also provide training for forensic scientists in many different countries.

Back at the laboratory

After the crime scene has been cleared, evidence is brought back to a laboratory for further investigation. Here the forensic scientists start to look for clues that will help the police link the crime to the criminal. The clues that they are looking for include traces of blood, sweat or fingerprints. In addition, fibres from clothes or a single hair can help establish that someone was at a crime scene. Forensic scientists test any weapons found either at the scene of the crime, or in the homes of suspects. If the crime is a murder, the body of the victim will undergo a post-mortem. This means looking for external

◀ *Evidence being gathered from a crime scene by forensic scientists. They are wearing special suits, called clean suits, over their clothes to make sure that they do not contaminate the crime scene. The yellow numbered cards mark out important pieces of evidence.*

► *A scene from the popular television drama about the work of forensic scientists, CSI: New York.*

marks on the body or even cutting the body open to look at the internal organs. The examination is performed by a forensic pathologist (see pages 14–15). The aim is to establish the cause and time of death.

Forensics on television

Police dramas on television have always been very popular with viewers. In the past few years, dramas that concentrate on the work of forensic scientists have been broadcast around the world. One of the first forensic dramas was the American show *Quincy M.E.* which started broadcasting in 1976. Since then there has been the hit American show *CSI: Crime Scene Investigation,* whilst British television has produced *Silent Witness* and *Waking the Dead.* These television shows have created a lot of interest in the work of forensic scientists. However, they have also caused something called the 'CSI Effect' where the general public expect forensic science to be able to solve all crimes (which it can't) and to do so incredibly fast, as shown on television.

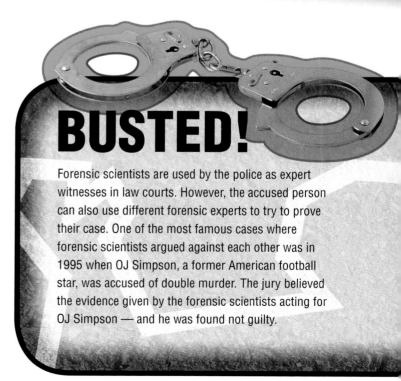

BUSTED!

Forensic scientists are used by the police as expert witnesses in law courts. However, the accused person can also use different forensic experts to try to prove their case. One of the most famous cases where forensic scientists argued against each other was in 1995 when OJ Simpson, a former American football star, was accused of double murder. The jury believed the evidence given by the forensic scientists acting for OJ Simpson — and he was found not guilty.

FINGERPRINTING

In 1891, the Argentinian police were the first police force to use fingerprints to catch criminals. Now police forces worldwide keep detailed records of fingerprints and employ scientists who are experts at finding them. Every individual has their own unique fingerprints which are the patterns of ridges in the skin of the fingertips. This means that if the police have fingerprint evidence, it becomes much easier to solve a crime.

Leaving a trace

Whenever a person's skin touches a surface it leaves behind a faint mark. With fingerprints this is usually a print made from the sweat or grease that lies on the surface of the skin. In addition, if someone has a liquid, such as blood or ink, on their fingertips, this can leave fingerprints at the crime scene. A fingerprint that is visible to the naked eye is called a patent print, whilst one that appears invisible is a latent print.

When a crime scene has been secured (see pages 8, 12 and 13), the forensic scientists have to look for any fingerprints that have been left behind. If they are searching for latent fingerprints they will use a fine brush with powder. The powder will stick to the sweat left behind. This is then lifted off using adhesive tape and taken back to the laboratory for analysis. Evidence taken back to the laboratory will also be tested for fingerprints.

▲ Taking fingerprints is one of the most important parts of investigating a crime scene. This forensic scientist is brushing powder over the glass of a window, checking for fingerprints.

FACT FILE

Fingerprints are usually a reliable way of catching criminals. However, occasionally mistakes are made. In 1997 Stephan Cowan was arrested for a shooting in Boston, USA, after a fingerprint was found at the scene of the crime that appeared to match his. Cowan protested his innocence but was sent to prison. Eventually the police agreed to analyse his fingerprints again. The investigation showed that the forensic laboratory that held Cowan's fingerprints had accidentally put the murderer's name label on his fingerprints. After serving six years in prison, Cowan was released.

Matching the prints

Once fingerprints have been found, they have to be compared with all the fingerprints that the police have on record. This is done by looking for similarities between the two prints. The more similarities that exist, the more likely it becomes that the prints are the same. Today there are computer programs that can compare fingerprints, speeding up the process.

Looking on the database

Fingerprints are only useful as evidence if the police are able to match any fingerprints found at a crime scene to fingerprints that they have on their records. Most countries now have the fingerprint records of everybody who has been convicted of a crime. Some countries, including Great Britain, retain the fingerprint records of anybody who has been arrested for a recordable crime. This causes unease for some who see it as an attack on personal privacy and freedom. Others think that everybody's fingerprint records should be taken so that there are no gaps in the records.

ON TARGET

In the United States of America, the Federal Bureau of Investigation (FBI) maintains the Integrated Automated Fingerprint Identification System. This is a computer database with the fingerprints of over 55 million Americans. It is available to police forces across the US and can usually make a match within two hours.

▼ *When somebody is fingerprinted in a police station it is important that all ten fingerprints are taken. This is because each finger has a slightly different fingerprint pattern.*

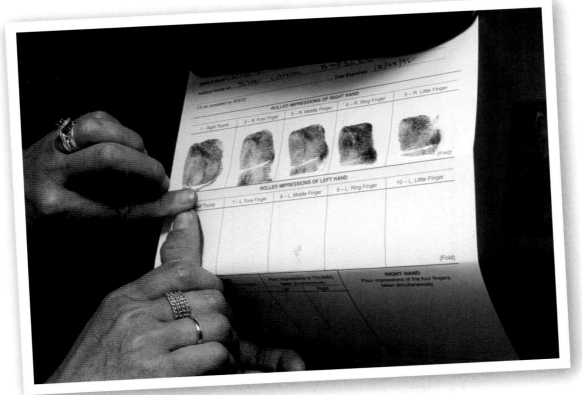

SECURING THE CRIME SCENE

When forensic science was in its infancy it was usually police officers who looked for evidence at the scene of a crime. There was no attempt to make the area secure. Police officers would walk around the crime scene and handle evidence without any supervision. As forensic science developed, it became more important that the whole area was closely controlled.

The 'Golden Hour'

When the police arrive at the scene of a major crime, such as a murder, they make sure that there is no one in danger and that any injured are being treated. At that point they cordon off the area and only allow in authorised personnel, such as forensic scientists. Speed is now important. Police officers need to question any witnesses while their memories are still clear. Evidence must be preserved by forensic scientists before it is altered by weather or time. This is known as the 'Golden Hour'.

▼ *Although speed is important for forensic scientists, the crime scene is preserved for as long as possible so that more detailed investigations can take place. An outline of the victim's body has been drawn so that the forensic scientists can remember how the body fell.*

ON TARGET

In August 2005, Hurricane Katrina passed through the American city of New Orleans, causing terrible floods. In the days that followed, over 700 people died. After the flood waters retreated, forensic investigators were brought in to confirm that the dead had been killed by the storm. As a result of their investigations they began several murder enquiries since some of the deaths looked suspicious.

Recording the scene

Once the forensic scientists arrive at a crime scene, they start to record all of the evidence that they can find. They take photographs of the scene from every angle, draw a map of the area marking anything that they think is relevant to the police investigation and collect evidence to take back to the laboratory. Sometimes police officers are used to make a thorough search to look for clues. They have to crawl along on their hands and knees looking for potential evidence. In some crimes, the police do not know what they are looking for, but anything found is recorded in case it turns out to be important in later investigations.

▲ *Securing an outside crime scene needs to be done at a fast pace because the changing weather and pollution may contaminate the evidence very quickly. Each yellow letter is linked to a piece of evidence that has been taken away.*

Dressing for the scene

Whenever anybody walks on to a crime scene they will leave something behind such as fibres from their clothes, mud from their shoes or even some hair. Any of these might contaminate the crime scene and slow down the investigation. Everybody who enters the crime scene should wear a clean suit which covers them from head to foot. They should also wear special shoes or overshoes to prevent contamination and to help identify their footprints.

BUSTED!

In November 2008 a British man called Peter Mahoney was arrested for an armed carjacking. When the burnt-out car was found, forensic scientists discovered some hairs that had survived the flames. These hairs had come from a dog. When Mahoney was arrested, a vet took a hair sample from his dog, Buster. The hair matched the hairs found in the car. This forensic evidence was used to link Mahoney to the crime. He was found guilty and jailed for four years.

THE POST-MORTEM

A post-mortem (or after-death) examination, or autopsy, takes place in order to find out why somebody has died, especially if their death was sudden or suspicious. Post-mortems are also used to identify a body if it has been badly burnt in a fire or if the body has decomposed. These examinations are carried out by specialists called forensic pathologists.

External examination

When a body is brought into an autopsy room, an assessment of the body is made. The forensic pathologist will look for clues such as cuts, bruises or other marks on the skin. Every mark will be recorded with photos and written notes. If there are stab wounds or bullet holes on the body they are studied as well. These wounds can show what angle the dead person was attacked at, and how deep the wound went. In many cases an external examination is only the start of the investigation, as more clues about somebody's death can be found inside the body.

FACT FILE

One of the main purposes of a post-mortem is to determine the cause of death. This is especially important if the death appears suspicious. The pathologist will make a detailed examination of the outside and the inside of the body. The post-mortem should reveal whether the victim died of natural causes (old age or undiagnosed illness), was murdered, committed suicide or died accidentally. On some rare occasions no cause of death can be found.

▼ Pathologists carry out a post-mortem. A post-mortem is performed to establish the cause of death or to increase the knowledge of a fatal disease.

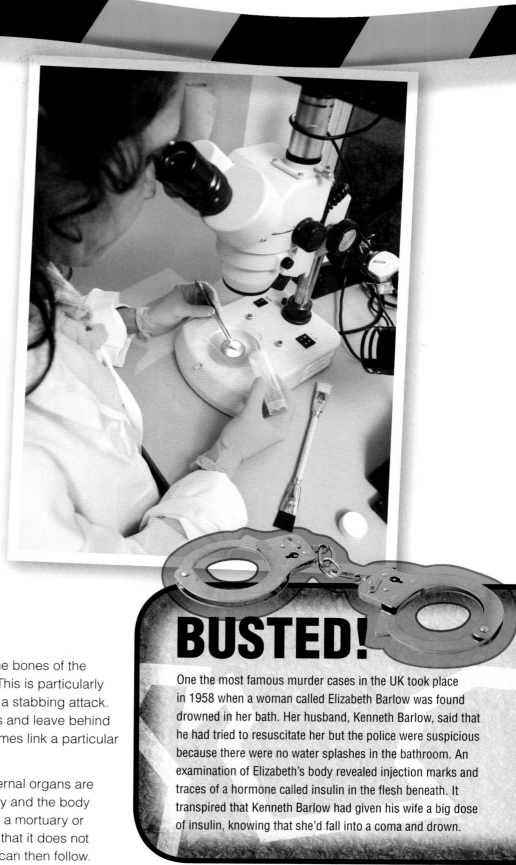

► *Examining bones under a microscope can give many clues as to the cause of death. A stabbing or a shooting can damage bones and it may be possible to match this damage to a weapon.*

Opening up the body

When all the information from an external examination has been recorded, the pathologist will start an examination of the internal organs of the body. Pathologists use special saws to cut through the rib cage. After this the organs, such as the heart, lungs and stomach, can be removed for closer examination. Half-digested food inside the stomach will tell the pathologist the last thing that somebody ate before they died and how long it had been in the stomach. This can help to establish a time of death.

One major cause of violent death is bleeding inside the skull after a heavy blow to the head. To find out if this did cause death, the brain has to be removed and examined.

Along with the internal organs, the bones of the dead can also reveal evidence. This is particularly useful when looking at victims of a stabbing attack. Stab wounds can damage bones and leave behind a mark. These marks can sometimes link a particular weapon to the stabbing.

Once the autopsy is over, the internal organs are carefully replaced inside the body and the body is sewn up. The body is stored in a mortuary or morgue at a low temperature, so that it does not decompose. Burial or cremation can then follow.

BUSTED!

One the most famous murder cases in the UK took place in 1958 when a woman called Elizabeth Barlow was found drowned in her bath. Her husband, Kenneth Barlow, said that he had tried to resuscitate her but the police were suspicious because there were no water splashes in the bathroom. An examination of Elizabeth's body revealed injection marks and traces of a hormone called insulin in the flesh beneath. It transpired that Kenneth Barlow had given his wife a big dose of insulin, knowing that she'd fall into a coma and drown.

15

NATURAL CLUES: INSECTS

When somebody dies, their body starts to release foul-smelling chemicals, such as cadaverine and putrescine. These chemicals attract insects to the corpse. Some of these insects will eat the decaying flesh that they find. Other insects will lay eggs on the corpse so that their newly-hatched young will have a ready supply of food. Experts called forensic entomologists study these insects and use them to work out when somebody died.

The arrival of the insects

The first insects to arrive at a dead body are usually flies. There are many different types of fly, including blowflies or house flies, which will use a dead body as a host for their eggs. The emerging maggots can then feed on the body. About a week later, beetles and mites follow. These insects will either lay their eggs on the body, eat the decomposing flesh or eat the maggots that are on the body. As the body reaches the final stages of decomposition, clothes moths are attracted to the body to feed on the corpse's hair or fur. The presence (or absence) of these different insects can help to establish the time of death.

▶ *Whenever anything living dies it immediately becomes a source of food for insects or their young. Maggots swarm over this decaying sheep's head.*

BUSTED!

Evidence from forensic entomology was used during the trial of David Westerfield of San Diego, California, USA, in 2002. He stood accused of murdering seven-year-old Danielle Van Dam. Both the prosecution and the defence used forensic entomologists to determine when Danielle Van Dam died. They disagreed about the age of fly larvae found on the body of Danielle. The prosecution won the case and Westerfield was found guilty.

▼ *One of the ways in which forensic entomologists can determine the time of a death is to identify the flies that have settled on the body, and what stage of their life cycle has been reached. Some flies are taken back to the laboratory for further examination under a microscope.*

Life cycles

Forensic entomologists study the life cycles of insects. An adult fly will lay her eggs around any openings in the dead body, such as the ears or nose. In 24 hours these will hatch into maggots (larvae). As the maggots feed on the corpse, they grow and moult their skin twice. After about ten days the maggots turn into pupae. This stage lasts about a week and then the adult flies emerge. These flies are ready to lay their own eggs in just one day. So if a forensic entomologist finds the pupae, for instance, of a particular fly on a dead body, it helps to establish a possible time of death.

Other crimes

As well as murder enquiries, forensic entomologists are used in several different types of criminal investigation. They can be used when the police are investigating the neglect of animals, or the neglect of vulnerable people such as children or the elderly. They can also be used to investigate illegal goods. Any insects on these goods could tell the police where the goods first came from.

ON TARGET

In 1995 police in Canada became concerned that bears were being shot so that their gall bladders could be removed. They believed that the gall bladders were being smuggled to Asia to be used in traditional medicine. In July 1995 two dead bears were found. The insects on the bodies were investigated to establish a time of death. This evidence helped link the bears' deaths to two men who were in the area at the time when the bears were known to have died.

SOILS AND SEEDS

Natural materials, such as soil, seeds or pollen, can be very useful to forensic scientists. Many of these materials stick to people very easily, especially on their shoes and clothes, and will also fall off. By analysing natural materials gathered from a crime scene, forensic scientists can sometimes find out where a murder took place and if a suspect was at the scene of the crime.

Different kinds of soil

Police can use experts called forensic geologists to study soil samples and other natural materials taken from a crime scene. There are many different kinds of soil, even within quite a small area, and other natural materials such as leaves or seeds can only be found in certain places and at certain times of the year. For instance, if a particular pollen spore is found at a crime scene forensic scientists can use it to identify a plant. Since each plant produces pollen at particular times of the year, pollen samples can give important clues about when the crime occurred and even the whereabouts of either the suspect or the victim.

BUSTED!

In September 2000 a woman and her son went missing in south Australia. Their car was found with a muddy shovel inside it, but with no sign of the two missing people. An analysis of the soil that was stuck to the blade of the shovel led the police to a quarry, where they found the buried bodies of the missing people. This evidence also led to the arrest of a man for the double murder.

▼ *Grains of pollen under a microscope. If pollen is found at a crime scene then simply identifying which plant the pollen came from helps to establish when a crime was committed.*

▼ *Boots and shoes can provide all sorts of clues for forensic scientists. Some of the more useful clues can be found on the soles. Soil and seeds can often be found stuck to shoes and may link a suspect to the scene of the crime, leading to an arrest.*

ON TARGET

In the United States the FBI has its own forensic science laboratory in Quantico, Virginia. One group of FBI scientists works at the Trace Evidence Unit. It analyses and compares any small materials found during a crime investigation. The Trace Evidence Unit works on about 2,000 cases every year.

Looking for materials

Forensic scientists looking for soil and seed clues will look in a variety of places, not just at the scene of a crime. If the crime is a murder, it may be that the victim was killed in one location and moved to another. Analysing samples from the victim's clothes, hair and fingernails might reveal where they died. A suspect's clothes, home and even their car may also be inspected in order to establish if they were at the scene of a crime at a particular time.

One of the first times that seeds helped convict a murder suspect was in 1942. Some grass seeds were found on the clothes of a murder suspect. A botanist looked at the seeds and discovered that the kind of grass the seeds came from was very rare and could only be found in a few places. One of those places was the scene of the murder. On top of that, the seeds were only produced in one month every year. It was the same month that the murder was committed.

USING BLOOD

Whenever a violent attack is being investigated by the police it is likely that there will be blood at the scene of the crime. This may be the blood of the victim or, if there was a struggle, of the attacker. Any blood found as part of a crime scene investigation will be examined as it can reveal all sorts of vital clues.

Testing the blood

If an attack took place some time before the police arrived, any blood at the scene would have dried out and would simply appear as a stain. Therefore the first thing that needs to be done is for an expert called a forensic serologist to test the stain for blood using the Kastle-Meyer Test. If the stain turns out to be blood, a sample is taken to the laboratory for further analysis.

In 1902 an Austrian scientist called Karl Landsteiner (see photo) discovered that human blood could be broken up into four main types: A, B, AB and O. This is known as the ABO grouping. Everybody's blood belongs to one of these groups. A laboratory can use a process called electrophoresis to establish to which group a blood sample belongs. However, because so many people share the same blood group it cannot be used by itself to prove someone's identity. It can help to narrow down the suspects, in the case of the attacker, or to help to identify the victim.

▼ *Karl Landsteiner's discovery of blood types not only helped forensic scientists with their work but also made blood transfusions possible. The first blood transfusion took place in 1907.*

◄ *Bloodstain patterns help forensic scientists to work out what was happening when the crime was committed.*

ON TARGET

In order to help US police forces find as many clues as they can from the scene of a crime, the FBI supports various groups of forensic scientists, allowing them to work together in the fight against crime. One of these groups is the Scientific Working Group on Bloodstain Pattern Analysis (SWGSTAIN). The members of this group are working towards improving bloodstain pattern analysis in order to develop it and solve more crimes.

Patterns of bloodstains

The shape of bloodstains at the scene of a crime can tell police a lot about what was happening when a crime was committed. The bloodstains can help to establish if the victim was moving when they were struck, and what kind of weapon was used to attack them. Forensic scientists usually call these stains 'blood spatter patterns'. A round spatter on the ground usually shows that blood is dripping straight down. However, if this spatter is over a wide area it is a sign that the blood has fallen from a height. A spray of tiny blood spatters on a wall indicates that the blood hit the wall hard, possibly after someone was hit with a heavy object or after a shooting.

DNA EVIDENCE

The use of DNA (deoxyribonucleic acid) fingerprinting has revolutionised the way in which police forces can solve crimes. DNA is made up of a long string of molecules inside every single cell in the human body. It carries information about how our bodies are built, such as height, hair colour and resistance to various diseases. Only identical twins or triplets carry the same DNA. Everybody else carries their own unique set of DNA molecules inside every cell. Scientists can use 'DNA fingerprints' to identify someone, just like actual fingerprints.

The invention of DNA fingerprinting

In 1985 Professor Sir Alec Jeffreys discovered a way to extract DNA from cells and compare it with another DNA set. Using this technique, it is possible to see whether DNA found at a crime scene matches that of anybody linked to a crime scene.

ON TARGET

Police forces around the world are building up databases of DNA fingerprints. This makes their jobs easier because if a DNA sample is found at a crime scene, they can simply make a comparison with all the DNA on file. The largest DNA database in the world is CODIS and is run by the FBI. The National DNA Database, the second largest in the world, is run by the UK's National Policing Improvement Agency. Between 1998 and 2010, over 300,000 crimes were detected with help from the DNA Database.

It was first used to solve two murders: one committed in 1983 and another in 1986. A man had confessed to both killings, but Jeffreys compared the man's DNA with some found at both murder scenes and proved that he did not commit the crimes. The same DNA sample eventually led to the arrest of another man.

◀ Any DNA fingerprints that are created from DNA samples have to be compared with a huge database of DNA fingerprints. The best way to do this is to turn the DNA fingerprint into a visual form so that a comparison can be made. Alec Jeffreys is shown here, comparing two DNA fingerprints.

Extracting DNA

Two years before Alec Jeffreys developed DNA fingerprinting, scientist Kary Mullis invented the Polymerase Chain Reaction (PCR) in the United States. This allowed scientists to isolate the specific piece of DNA that they were interested in and make as many copies of it as they needed. First, a forensic scientist takes a cell sample and purifies it to get rid of any impurities. It is then mixed with chemicals that extract the DNA. The sample is put into a PCR machine which 'amplifies' the DNA. This means that it makes copies of the DNA many thousands of times until there is enough DNA material for scientists to work with.

Short Tandem Repeat profiling

Once the DNA has been copied in the PCR machine, it has to be put into a visual form so that a comparison can be made. The most common technique for this is known as Short Tandem Repeat (STR) profiling. As with DNA fingerprinting, it allows a scientist to compare repeated short sections of DNA extracted from a DNA sample by turning it into

BUSTED!

In 1985 Kirk Bloodsworth was sentenced to death for the murder of Dawn Hamilton in Maryland, USA. Even though several witnesses placed him at the scene of the crime, he always said he was innocent. In 1992, after his death sentence had been turned into a life sentence, Bloodsworth's DNA was analysed and it was found that he was not the killer. Eleven years later the real killer was identified using DNA evidence.

long bar codes or graphs. Then the scientist can compare the different DNA samples to see which ones match.

▼ *The amount of DNA found at a crime scene is usually very small so it is important that the DNA is replicated. This is done using a Polymerase Chain Reaction machine. Each of the small tubes will create a new DNA set.*

BONES AND SKULLS

One group of forensic scientists are known as forensic anthropologists. They study human remains a long time after death has taken place. In the case of dead bodies, the bones and skull last long after the rest of the body has decomposed. Studying these bones can help to establish the age, sex, ethnic origin and cause of death of the dead person.

Studying the bones

If a dead body has been reduced to a skeleton, these remains are laid out for examination on a mortuary table. Because skeletons change throughout a person's life, it is possible to work out the age of the person who has died. Pelvic bones in men and women are a different size and shape so the gender of the skeleton can also be identified. The skull helps with finding out about the ethnic origin of the skeleton. The skulls of Europeans tend to be different from those of either Africans or Asians. However, skull shape is not always a reliable indicator of ethnic origin as there are wide variations within each ethnic group. If the bones show any signs of disease, that can help to identify individuals.

BUSTED!

In 1994 an Argentinian forensic anthropology team examined the 200 victims of a massacre that took place in the Guatemalan village of Dos Erres in 1982. Their findings led to the arrest of a Guatemalan soldier who was living in the United States in May 2010. He was charged with their murder.

▶ Forensic anthropologists at work in Bosnia-Herzegovina in 2005. They make detailed records before moving a skeleton from its burial site. In this case, their investigations helped to solve a war crime.

War crimes

One area of work for forensic anthropologists is in the field of solving war crimes. Since the 1990s there have been conflicts around the world where civilians have been rounded up, executed and buried in mass graves. Forensic anthropologists have worked in countries such as Rwanda, Kosovo, Bosnia-Herzegovina and various countries in South America (see box right). They examine the scattered bones found in these mass graves. Using these bones they can work out the time and cause of death. They also try to reunite as many bones as possible so that the bodies can be buried properly.

Waking the dead

Sometimes the only way to identify a dead person is to use the skull to reconstruct the face. Traditionally this is done by adding layers of clay to the skull. The amount of flesh and muscle to be added is done by using the same amount as would normally be seen on a person of the same age and sex. The person making the facial reconstruction has to make an educated guess about hair or skin colour. Today facial reconstructions are made using a computer and data from CT (computer tomography) scans of people with a similar skull size and shape. Facial details such as skin, eye colour and hair are added.

ON TARGET

The Argentine Forensic Anthropology Team works internationally on war crime and human rights cases. They have helped to identify individuals in Bolivia, El Salvador, Colombia, East Timor, Chile and the Lebanon. In each of these cases they were able to identify many of the victims of these crimes, so that family members could take them away for a proper burial.

▼ A forensic scientist reconstructs the features of a face. The scientist will have scanned the skull shape into the computer and built up layers of muscle digitally.

CASE STUDY: THE BODY FARM

The 'Body Farm' is officially called the Forensic Anthropology Center at the University of Tennessee, USA. It has proved an invaluable source of information for forensic scientists, particularly forensic anthropologists, around the world. The Body Farm studies the way that human bodies decompose in different kinds of environment. The results of these studies allow forensic anthropologists to make a more accurate assessment of the time of death.

The beginnings

The Forensic Anthropology Center was started in 1971 by William M. Bass. Bass had just started as Professor of Anthropology at the University of Tennessee and had become the first forensic anthropologist for the state of Tennessee. It was his forensic anthropology work that convinced him that more research was needed into how bodies decompose when they are placed in different environments – and so the Body Farm was born.

▼ Corpses in the Body Farm are wrapped up in different materials such as cloth or plastic. Each body is then checked to see how the materials have affected the way that the body has decomposed.

Inside the Body Farm

The Body Farm occupies an area of about 10,000 square metres. The whole area is surrounded by a high wall which is topped with razor wire. This is designed to keep out anybody who might break in and contaminate the bodies inside. In 2007 there were about 150 dead bodies inside the Center. Some of these are unidentified bodies from local morgues, but most of the bodies come from people who had agreed to donate their bodies to the Center after death. There are currently about 650 people who have agreed that the Center can use their bodies after death.

The work of the Body Farm

The bodies inside the Center are studied as they decompose. Bodies are covered in plastic sheets or are left exposed. They are placed in the full Sun or in the shade. Some of the bodies are buried, placed in a tub full of water or put into the boot of a car. Scientists at the Center watch carefully as the bodies begin to decay. They note down physical changes to the bodies, the amount of insect activity and the speed of decomposition. All of this information is entered onto a computer database. They have also begun to research the smells released during decomposition so that dogs can be trained to search for corpses.

ON TARGET

The Center has been so successful that there are plans to expand it to nearly 50,000 square metres. At the same time, new Body Farms have started in three more American universities. The different temperatures and local environments at these universities will mean that the results of their studies will differ from those in Tennessee.

◀ The current head of the Forensic Anthropology Center, Dr Richard Jantz. He helps many police forces with their crime scene investigations.

BUSTED!

In December 1993, in the United States, 'Big Mike' Rubenstein called the police to tell them that he had found the bodies of three of his relatives in a cabin. He said that he had visited the cabin in November but that it was empty. The police investigated the deaths and became suspicious, especially after Rubenstein swiftly applied for life insurance payments on his dead relatives. They called in staff from the Body Farm. Their knowledge of body decomposition showed that the people had been killed in November 1993. 'Big Mike' Rubenstein was convicted of their murders.

CLOTHES AND SHOES

It was the French forensic scientist Edmond Locard who created the principle that every forensic scientist knows – 'every contact leaves a trace'. In other words, whenever two people or materials touch, material is transferred from one to the other. This can include natural materials left behind on shoes or clothes, or the fibres that fall off a person's clothing.

Leaving a print

One of the things that forensic scientists look for when a crime scene is secured is shoe or boot prints. However, prints like these are not likely to remain fresh for long so it is vital that they are recorded quickly. First a cast of the print is made using a liquid plastic resin. When this hardens it is taken to the laboratory, where another cast is made from the resin cast. This time a hard material such as plaster-of-paris is used.

Once the cast of the shoe print is ready, it can be examined for clues. One of the things that forensic scientists look out for is any signs of wear and tear.

▲ *Examining prints left behind by boots and shoes can help to find out if a suspect was at the scene of a crime. Different shoes have different designs on their soles.*

ON TARGET

The FBI maintains a database of the prints made by shoe and boot soles and heels. This allows police forces to make a comparison between prints found at crime scenes and prints on the database. Fashions in shoes, especially trainers, change fast so it is important that shoe manufacturers let the FBI know about any new designs as they appear.

usually be unique to a particular shoe so it is fairly easy to match it to the suspect's shoes. If the scientist wants to know the make of shoe, they can look at the patterns on the sole and match it to one kind of shoe.

Comparing fibres

One type of clue that suspected criminals leave behind are fibres from their clothes. Clothes are made from different materials, such as cotton or wool, and have been dyed various colours. If any fibres are found at the scene of the crime they can be compared with fibres from the clothes of any suspects. This can be done with a comparison microscope. This is a kind of double microscope that allows two fibre samples to be viewed at the same time. If a match is made, this can help to place a suspect at a crime scene. If a forensic scientist has only one fibre to work with, he or she can use a FTIR (Fourier transform infrared spectroscopy) machine. This machine examines the fibre using different wavelengths of light. The result can then be compared to a database of materials.

BUSTED!

In December 2009, a 24-year-old man was arrested in Kansas, USA, after an armed robbery in a pizza restaurant. The robber had covered his face with a ski mask but he left his shoe prints on the restaurant's doormat. The police were able to match these prints with the shoe prints of one of their suspects.

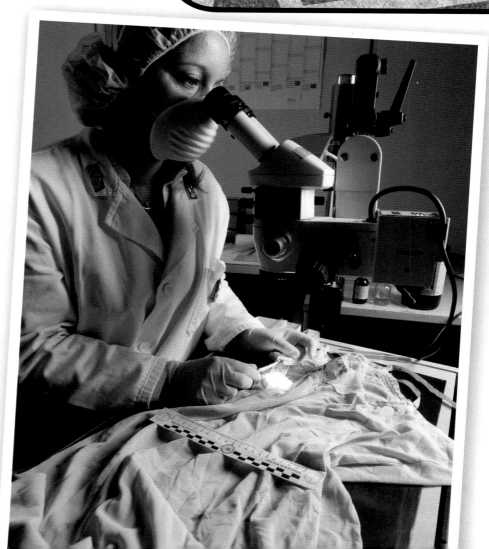

▶ A forensic scientist collects evidence from a blood-stained dress. She is using a microscope to collect single hairs or fibres from the dress.

PAPER TRAIL

Some crimes are almost impossible to spot. There are criminals who are experts at forgery, producing fake banknotes, documents or works of art. Forensic scientists work to uncover these forgeries. They also examine any pieces of paper at a crime scene, searching for hidden clues such as the impression of writing that cannot be seen by the naked eye.

▲ *Banknotes now contain all sorts of features that make them very difficult, or too expensive, for forgers to copy. Watermarks, microletters and thin metal strips are added to banknotes when they are being printed.*

Revealing the forgery

Banknotes are printed in special, highly secure buildings called mints. The banknotes that they produce are printed so that they are almost impossible to forge. However, this does not stop some criminals from printing their own money and trying to get them past people who are too busy or careless to check them properly. If a forensic scientist is given a banknote to examine, there are various things that he or she can look for.

Real banknotes use a type of paper that is difficult for the public to obtain. During the printing process microletters are added that can only be seen with a magnifying glass. There are also some features of the banknote that can only be seen under an ultraviolet light.

BUSTED!

The Chinese police broke up a banknote forgery ring in April 2009. At the start of the year fake banknotes were circulating around various regions in China. The fake notes had a face value of £17 million. After using forensic techniques which found that the forgeries used the wrong kind of paper, the Chinese police were able to seize the counterfeit cash and arrest over 600 people.

The age of paper, paint and ink

Forgeries of paintings, books or documents are sometimes difficult to detect. The materials used to create the forgery can be examined to determine when they were made. For instance, in 1981 the diaries of Adolf Hitler were 'discovered' by a journalist in Germany. Handwriting experts and a well-known historian said that the diaries were real. However, an examination by forensic experts found that the paper and ink used in the diaries were modern and were not available in Hitler's time. The journalist, Gerd Heidemann, and the forger, Konrad Kujau (see photo), were each given prison sentences for their part in the hoax.

The electrostatic detective

Whenever somebody writes on a notepad, a very faint copy of what was written is left on the sheet under the paper that was first used. If a forensic investigator is searching for hidden writing, he or she can use a machine called an ESDA (Electrostatic Detection Apparatus). A thin piece of film is laid over the paper and an electric charge is then passed through the film. The electrical charge is strongest on top of where the hidden writing is on the paper. Powder is then scattered over the film and the excess is blown away. The powder that is left behind will reveal the writing on the paper.

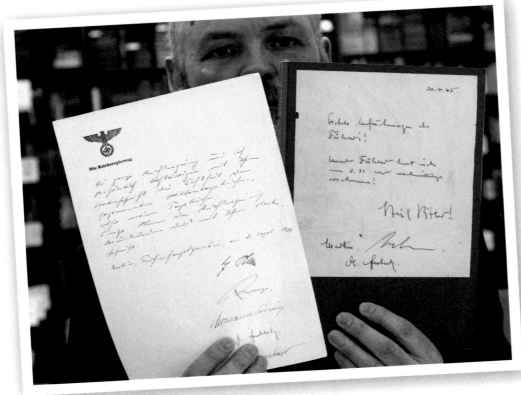

◄ The Hitler diaries were created by a forger called Konrad Kujau. He is shown holding letters that he said proved that the diaries were real. The letters, and the diary, were fakes and Kujau was sent to prison for 48 months.

GUNS AND BULLETS

If a gun is used during a crime then a lot of clues will be left behind, even if the gun has been taken away from the crime scene. As soon as the crime scene is secured, the forensic team start to search for evidence of the shooting that took place. These investigations continue in the laboratory.

Evidence at the crime scene

After a shooting incident, forensic scientists will look for evidence to help establish the exact location of the victim and the suspected shooter. They will examine the position of the body of the victim, any blood spattered around the crime scene, bullet holes, used bullets and bullet cases.

Blood spatters on a wall can show forensic experts from which direction the gun was fired. Any bullet cases will show the police where the gun was fired from. The position and angle of any bullet holes can also show where the gun shot came from.

ON TARGET

The UK's National Ballistic Intelligence Service was established to help enforce tough anti-gun laws and to reduce the number of gun-related crimes. In April 2008 it launched a national database of all firearms, bullets and bullet cases in the hands of the police. It also has three laboratories which are dedicated to examining firearms.

▼ A bullet hole in a tree trunk has been marked up by a forensic scientist. There is a vertical and a horizontal ruler so that the hole can be measured. The hole has been taped up to protect it from the weather.

▲ A forensic scientist examines the bottom of a bullet case, using his computer to view the magnified image.

Evidence in the laboratory

It is unusual for the gun used in a crime to have been left at the crime scene. However, the bullets and bullet cases found at the crime scene can be examined because different types of gun use different types of bullet. Identifying the bullet that was used by the criminal will narrow down the types of gun that could have been used to fire the bullet.

When a bullet is fired out of a gun, grooves inside the barrel of the gun leave marks on the bullet. These marks are called striations. The firing pin inside the gun also leaves a small hole in the bullet case. Like fingerprints or DNA, the marks and holes are unique to each gun and the same striations are left every time the gun is fired.

The shooting bath

If the suspect of a shooting is found with a gun it is imperative to find out if this was the same gun that was used. The gun is brought to the forensic laboratory where it is fired into a large tank filled with water for safety, and in order to collect the

fired bullet. Using a comparison microscope, the scientists can then compare the bullets and cases fired in the laboratory with any bullets and cases found at the crime scene. If the striations and holes are the same, they know that they have the gun used at the crime.

BUSTED!

In April 2010, 39-year-old Stephan J Tamburo III of West Virginia, USA, was arrested for the murder of his father. The murder took place in December 2008 but the body was not found until April 2009. DNA samples from the body proved the identity of the victim and bullets in the body were matched to a gun in his son's home.

DRUGS AND POISONS

If drug use or poisons are suspected in a crime, scientists called toxicologists are called in to help to identify the toxins used. A toxin is any substance harmful to the human body. Toxicologists analyse unknown powders or liquids to identify drugs, as well as substances or poisons used to kill someone.

Drugs and crime

Most drug crime is linked to the production, trafficking and selling of illegal drugs. In order to bring drug criminals to court, law enforcement agencies often use the skills of toxicologists to analyse substances found on the suspect, or at the crime scene, in order to prove guilt. In addition, driving under the influence of drugs or alcohol is against the law. Levels of alcohol or drugs in the body can be tested using roadside tests. Police may take saliva, urine or blood samples from a suspect for further analysis by a toxicologist.

◄ Bottles of arsenic and capsicum from the 1920s. The bottle on the left, containing arsenic, is a special shape and colour, with the word 'poison' embossed in the glass, for ease of identification. The one on the right does not contain poison.

BUSTED!

Britain's most prolific mass murderer was Dr Harold Shipman. It is believed that he killed over 250 people that were in his care. The police became involved after it was noticed that a large number of his patients were dying. An examination of his last victim found a large amount of a drug called diamorphine in her body. Shipman was eventually convicted of the murder of 15 more of his patients, who all died after a drug overdose administered by their own GP, Dr Shipman.

Killing with poison

In the past, poison was one of the most favoured ways of killing a victim. Poisons, such as arsenic, strychnine and antimony, were all used to commit murder. With today's sophisticated forensic sciences it would be very difficult for anybody to get away with murder by poisoning. However, in 1978, Georgi Markov, a Bulgarian communist defector living in London, was killed by poisoning. On his way to work in 1978, he felt a jab in the leg. He turned to see somebody pick up an umbrella and walk away. Three days later Markov was dead. A tiny pellet containing the poison ricin was found in his body. The pellet had been stabbed into him with the umbrella. His killer was never caught as the Bulgarian authorities denied any knowledge of the murder and refused to co-operate.

Testing for toxins

An important part of a forensic toxicologist's job is to identify any drugs or poisons linked to a crime by testing unknown substances found at the crime scene, or detecting drugs or poisons in body fluids, tissues or organs. One of the best ways of doing this is to use a mass spectrometer which rapidly screens for a range of drugs and poisons, even if they are present in tiny quantities. It does this by breaking a substance up into its separate molecules. Once the molecules are separated, they can be examined and any toxins can be identified.

▼ *A chemist places samples in a mass spectrometer in order to identify all the substances contained in each sample.*

ON TARGET

Police forces around the world have specialist forensic teams that are experts in toxicology. The FBI has a Chemistry Unit which works in the field of toxicology. They have specialist equipment that is not normally available to police forces and they assist at crime scenes where the use of poisons is suspected.

CRASH INVESTIGATIONS

Any major crash that involves transport is always investigated to see if the cause of the crash can be established. Forensic scientists have to discover if the crash was accidental or deliberate, or was caused by carelessness. They do this by gradually piecing together the chain of events that led to the crash.

Car crashes

If there is a car crash or an incident that involves several vehicles, one of the things that the forensic scientists will look for are the skid marks on the road. The skid marks are caused when drivers suddenly brake but the vehicles keep moving. The length of a skid mark can show how fast the vehicle was travelling at the time of the crash. A wobbly skid mark suggests that the driver was not in control of his or her vehicle. If the skid marks start too close to an obstruction, they may indicate that the driver was not paying attention whilst driving. Forensic investigators can also recreate crashes using crash test dummies.

▼ *The skid marks on a road can show what each vehicle was doing when a crash took place.*

ON TARGET

There are several private companies that specialise in investigating car crashes. Businesses, such as Crash Forensics in Kansas, USA, work with both the police service and insurance companies to find out how a crash actually took place. Along with skid marks they also analyse the vehicles in the crash and even create a computer-generated reconstruction of the crash.

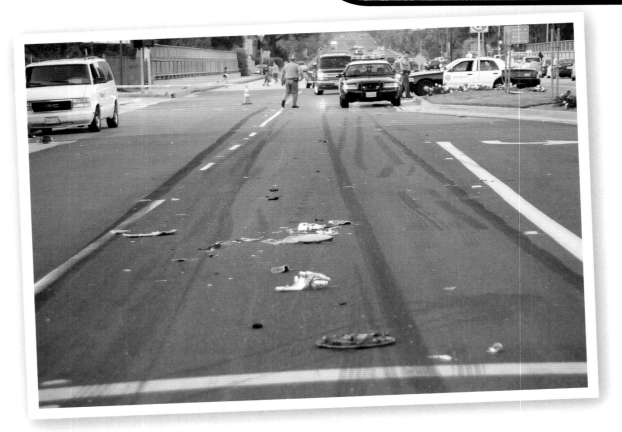

Train and plane crashes

Whenever a train or plane crashes, the area of the crash is treated in the same way as a crime scene. The whole area is cordoned off and only authorised personnel are allowed inside. The job of the forensic team is to establish the cause of the crash. This is normally a complicated job as the crash could have happened because of faults in the body of the train or plane, negligence by a crew member or may even be a terrorist attack. For instance, in June 1998 a train crash in Germany killed over 100 people. It was eventually discovered that the crash was caused by metal fatigue in a single wheel.

The black box

At the site of a plane crash one of the first things that happens is the search for the 'black box'. In fact, every commercial plane has two boxes on board. One of them is a Cockpit Voice Recorder (CVR) which records conversations among the crew (see box right). The other is the Flight Data Recorder (FDR) which stores data from the plane's

BUSTED!

One of the planes involved in the 9/11 attacks on the United States in 2001 crashed in a field in Pennsylvania. There were no survivors. Forensic teams found the Cockpit Voice Recorder. From the recording they discovered that the passengers on the plane had attempted to overpower the hijackers. Just prior to the crash, one hijacker told another (who was acting as pilot) to crash the aircraft, in order to prevent the passengers from regaining control of it.

instruments. The material in these two boxes is invaluable in determining the cause of a plane crash. Both boxes are usually a bright red or orange colour so that they can be found easily.

◀ Crash investigators, wearing protective suits, examine a train crash in California, USA.

FIRE INVESTIGATIONS

Discovering the cause of a fire, the reasons why it spread and why people in the fire died is a difficult process. The fire will destroy a lot of the evidence needed in order to find out what actually happened. However, after a fire has been put out, firefighters work with the police and forensic scientists to establish what happened.

The cause of the fire

Fires nearly always start in one place, which is known as the 'seat'. Fires tend to travel upwards and then spread out. This makes it easier for the police to discover where the fire actually started. Fire damage will usually be greater as the investigators get closer to the seat.

Finding the seat of the fire means that it is easier to discover what caused the fire to start in the first place. Fire investigators will search through all of the burnt material at the seat to see if it was that which started the fire. Samples of charred debris are taken back to the laboratory to see if they will yield any clues. One of the things that they will look

BUSTED!

In February 2009 the Australian state of Victoria suffered one of the worst bushfires in Australian history. There were more than 12 separate major fires and about 400 smaller ones. Over 2,000 houses were destroyed and over 400 people lost their lives. Several people were arrested on suspicion of starting some of the fires deliberately, but only one person, Brendan Sokaluk, has been charged with arson and with causing the death of 11 people.

▶ Once a fire has been put out, the fire investigators will enter the remains of the fire-damaged area and begin to discover where the fire started and how it began.

for is traces of an accelerant. Accelerants are flammable liquids such as petrol or paint thinner. The presence of an accelerant would suggest that the fire was started on purpose.

▲ *Some materials burn more easily than others. Until recently, the foam used in soft furniture, such as sofas, was extremely flammable and meant that fires could spread very quickly.*

Fire testing

Forensic scientists do a large amount of work in the laboratory to see which materials burn most quickly and which give off the most smoke and toxic gases. A smoke density chamber will measure how much smoke is produced by any burning material. This knowledge is vital because smoke is a killer and forensic scientists can advise companies that create and furnish buildings about which materials produce the least smoke.

A cone calorimeter is a machine that tests the amount of heat materials give off when they burn, and also measures the speed at which the heat is created. This is important because the more heat a fire produces, the more intense the fire will be and the faster it spreads.

ON TARGET

Many firefighting teams have specialists within them that can work with the police and forensic scientists at the site of a fire. Many of these specialists use dogs known as 'Fire Investigation Dogs'. These dogs are trained to search out any suspected accelerants. The British government has published guidelines on how to train these dogs.

CASE STUDY: THE LOCKERBIE BOMBING

On Wednesday, 21 December, 1988, Pan Am Flight 103 took off from London's Heathrow Airport. Its destination was New York's John F. Kennedy International Airport. Just a few minutes after 7 pm, as the plane was flying over southern Scotland, the plane exploded. All 243 passengers and 16 crew members died instantly. Debris from the plane fell on the small Scottish town of Lockerbie and killed another 11 people, bringing the total number of fatalities to 270. The Air Accidents Investigation Branch immediately began to investigate the disaster.

Searching for clues

Over the next few months, over 1,000 police officers and soldiers carried out a fingertip search of the fields and forests around Lockerbie, gathering up the remains of the plane. They were told, "If it isn't growing and it isn't a rock, pick it up." They found over 10,000 items that came from the plane. Evidence of an explosive device was also found, so the investigators knew that the plane had been brought down by a bomb.

◄ This picture shows the fragments of the suitcase that contained the bomb that blew up Pan Am Flight 103 (see page 41). These fragments helped forensic scientists discover what the bomb was made of and how it was set to explode.

ON TARGET

The Air Accidents Investigation Branch was responsible for finding out how and why the plane had crashed. However, the suitcase and its contents were investigated by both British and American forensic teams. The American team came from the FBI and the British team were part of the Defence Evaluation and Research Agency (DERA).

Reconstructing the plane

All of the parts of the recovered aircraft were taken to Farnborough Airport, the headquarters of the Air Accidents Investigation Branch. There the remains of the plane were put back together again. The investigators found that an area on the left-hand side of the forward cargo hold had been completely ripped apart. This told them that the bomb had been placed there.

Reconstructing the bomb

Fifty-six pieces of highly-charred suitcase were also found. Investigators established that this was the suitcase that held the bomb. Forensic scientists traced tiny amounts of plastic explosives on the fragments of the suitcase to a factory in the Czech Republic. Pieces of a circuit board and a cassette player were also found. This was important because it was known that the same type of cassette player was used by Middle Eastern terrorist groups in bomb-making. Clothing fragments from the suitcase were analysed and traced back to Malta and it was this that first pointed to Libyan involvement. Later investigations in Malta showed that these clothes had been bought by Abdelbaset Al Megrahi.

BUSTED!

The Libyan government handed over Abdelbaset Al Megrahi to the British authorities in April 1999. He was tried at a special court in the Netherlands with four Scottish judges. The main evidence against Al Megrahi came from the Maltese shopkeeper who had sold him the clothes found at the crash site. He was found guilty and sentenced to life imprisonment. In August 2009 he was released after it was found that he had cancer.

Alleged to be a Libyan intelligence officer, Al Megrahi, who was chief of security for Libyan Arab Airlines, has been the only person to be convicted for the bombing.

◄ *The reconstructed remains of Pan Am Flight 103 are still housed in a warehouse by the Air Accidents Investigation Branch.*

GLOSSARY

Anthropology The scientific study of the biological origins and customs of different groups of people.

Autopsy A medical examination of a corpse in order to find out the cause of death.

Ballistics The study of the firing and movement of bullets.

Black box There are two black boxes on each commercial plane that record information about each flight. They are used to understand why planes crash.

Blood groups The division of human blood into four groups based on the absence or presence of chemicals in red blood cells.

Blood spatter patterns The shape of bloodstains at the scene of a crime.

Carjack To hijack a car or other vehicle.

Clean suit A special item of clothing that covers forensic investigators from head to foot to prevent contamination of the crime scene.

Comparison microscope A double microscope that allows two samples to be viewed at the same time.

Contaminate At a crime scene, contaminate means mixing evidence up with unwanted substances.

Counterfeit Imitation or forgery.

Database A comprehensive collection of data, such as fingerprints or DNA, that is stored on a computer.

Decomposition When a dead body starts to decay.

DNA A long string of molecules found inside the cell. It carries information about each individual. Each DNA string is unique to that individual.

DNA fingerprinting Also known as DNA profiling. Identifying somebody from DNA evidence.

Entomology The scientific study of insects.

Expert witness A person who is a specialist in a subject and is asked to present his or her expert opinion at a trial even though he or she was not at a crime.

Federal Bureau of Investigation (FBI) The Federal Bureau of Investigation is part of the US Department of Justice. It conducts investigations into major crimes and helps local police forces with their work.

Fibre A fine thread or strand.

Forgery Making a copy of something and then claiming it is genuine.

Geologist Somebody who studies rocks and soils.

'Golden Hour' The short period of time when a crime scene has not been altered by the weather or human activity.

Insulin A hormone produced by the pancreas, which regulates blood sugar levels. People with diabetes have to inject insulin into their bodies. An overdose can kill.

Larva(e) The stage of an insect's life cycle after it has hatched from an egg. Also called maggot.

Metal fatigue Gradual damage to the structure (and strength) of a piece of metal.

Molecule A group of chemically combined atoms.

Pathologist Somebody who studies diseases and injuries through an examination of the organs of the body.

Polymerase Chain Reaction A method for making copies of a DNA sample so that there is enough DNA to sample.

Post-mortem Another word for autopsy (see above).

Pupa(e) The stage of an insect's life cycle before it turns into an adult, and after the larval stage.

Short Tandem Repeat analysis A technique for turning information from a DNA sample into a visual form so that a comparison can be made.

Striations The unique marks left on a bullet that has been fired.

Toxicology The scientific study of poisonous chemicals.

Wavelength (of light) Light travels as waves. Different types of light have different wavelengths. Some are visible to the human eye and others, such as ultra violet light, are not.

FURTHER INFORMATION

Books

Carol Ballard, *Forensic Science*, Franklin Watts, 2010

Chris Cooper, *Forensic Science*, Dorling Kindersley, 2008

Elizabeth Dowen, *What's it Like to be a Forensic Scientist?*, A&C Black Publishers, 2009

Alex Frith, *Forensic Science*, Usborne Books, 2007

Douglas Lyle, *Forensics for Dummies*, John Wiley, 2004

Pete Moore, *The Forensics Handbook*, Eye Books, 2004

Richard Platt, *Forensics*, Kingfisher, 2008

Lisa Yount, *Forensic Science: From Fibers to Fingerprints*, Facts on File Inc, 2006

Websites

www.exploreforensics.co.uk
A British website that explores the world of forensics.

www.forensic-science-society.org.uk/information/careers.html
Information for young people who want to work in forensic science.

http://forensics.rice.edu
Background scientific information to the CSI series with plenty of online activities.

www.glasgowsciencecentre.org/forensicscience.aspx
Games involving forensic science from the Glasgow Science Centre.

www.centredessciencesdemontreal.com/stzatic/autopsy/flash.html
Solve a murder using forensic techniques. A website from the Montreal Science Centre.

http://video.nationalgeographic.com/video/player/science/health-human-body-sci/human-body/body-farm-sci.html
A short video on the National Geographic website, showing the work of the Body Farm in Tennessee, USA.

www.yourdiscovery.com/crime/_home/index.shtml
Forensic science from the Discovery Channel website.

Note to parents and teachers: every effort has been made by the Publishers to ensure that these websites are suitable for children, that they are of the highest educational value, and that they contain no inappropriate or offensive material. However, because of the nature of the Internet, it is impossible to guarantee that the contents of these sites will not be altered. We strongly advise that Internet access is supervised by a responsible adult.

INDEX

SERIES CONTENTS

Cybercrime Hacking • Case study: Gary McKinnon • Phishing • Cyberbullying • Cyberstalking • Virus attacks • Malware • Social networking sites • Fraudulent websites • Denial-of-service attacks • Identity theft • Case study: Pirate Bay • Cyberterrorism • Cyberwars • Case study: Cyberwars in Eastern Europe • Cybersecurity

Drug crime Worldwide drug problem • Which drugs are illegal? • Who are the criminals? • The flow of drugs • The cost of drugs • Tackling the traffickers • Smuggling and mules • Below the waves • Stop and search • Global drug watch • Surveillance • Operation Junglefowl • Going undercover • Drug bust • Operation Habitat • Drugs on the street • The future of drug crime

Forensics Inside picture • Fingerprinting • Securing the crime scene • The post-mortem • Natural clues: insects • Soil and seeds • Using blood • DNA evidence • Bones and skulls • Case study: The Body Farm • Clothes and shoes • Paper trail • Guns and bullets • Drugs and poisons • Crash investigations • Fire investigations • Case study: The Lockerbie bombing

People trafficking Defining people trafficking • History of people trafficking • The traffickers • The victims • Forced labour • The sex industry • Trafficking children • Source countries • In transit • Border controls • Case study: The European Union • Catching the criminals • Loopholes in the law • Police and welfare • Working with NGOs • Raising awareness • Taking a stand

Gun crime Defining gun crime • Which guns are used? • Who commits gun crime? • Case study: killing spree • How much gun crime is there? • Gun dealing • Gun control • Arming the police • Case study: Ganglands • Solving gun crime • Firearms in the crime lab • Case study: Washington snipers • Combating gun crime • Operation Trident • Gun crime in the media • Firearms debate

Youth crime What is youth crime? • The extent of youth crime • The causes of youth crime • Guns and knives • Case study: Columbine • Drugs and youth crime • Street gangs and crews • Case study: the Bloods and the Crips • Anti-social behaviour • Youth crime in the past • Fighting youth crime • Custodial sentences • Restorative justice • Community supervision • Young victims • Media scares • The way forward

Kidnapping and piracy Inside picture • In the past • Piracy at sea • Somalia • Case study: The MV Sirius Star • Policing the pirates • International law • Kidnapping for ransom • Abducting children • Taken hostage • Case study: Terry Waite • Hijacking • Negotiation • Armed response • Case study: Flight 93 • Training and support • Surviving kidnap and piracy

Policing and justice Criminal justice • Tackling crime • Officers on the street • National/international police • Police culture • Case study: police racism • Who guards the guardians? • Case study: A new police force • The justice system • Arrest and detention • The courts • Crime and punishment • Community sentences • Case study: terrorism • Victims • Young offenders • Changes to the system